The F... Word A

Turning Frustration into l _ ____.

Opportunities for Business Success

Eduardo J. Estrada

The F... Word Advantage

Eduardo J. Estrada

Published by Eduardo J. Estrada, 2023.

THE F... WORD ADVANTAGE

First edition. April 24, 2023.

ISBN: 979-8215100622

Written by Eduardo J. Estrada.

Table of Contents

This Book is dedicated to my Family, Parents and All who are finding solutions from frustrations for a better world.

Introduction

IN THIS BOOK, WE EXPLORE the concept of frustration and how it can be turned into an opportunity for improvement. Frustration is a normal human emotion, and it can lead to significant improvements in our personal and professional lives.

We all experience frustration, whether it's our kids struggling with their homework or managers dealing with unreliable suppliers. This book is your guide to transforming frustration into a state of flow and a great experience.

This book was originated from countless of situations, during my Lean Manufacturing journey, where I could see how Frustration could be converted in an improvement opportunity.

One of the key principles of Lean Manufacturing is the concept of continuous improvement. This means that any form of frustration or inefficiency in the production process is seen as an opportunity for improvement. Lean Manufacturing encourages businesses to continuously review their processes and eliminate waste, making them more efficient and effective.

Frustration is a natural part of any process or business. However, by applying the principles of Lean Manufacturing, frustration can be transformed into an opportunity for improvement, leading to better processes, higher-quality products, and more satisfied customers.

As a professional or business owner, you may be dealing with the frustration of a customer, unreliable suppliers, a difficult project, a challenging colleague, unexpected setbacks, limited options in the market, a complex environment or a team that's not satisfied. But imagine having a frustration-free environment that's efficient and accurate. Imagine having the confidence that you have the right team, products, and systems in place.

But how do we know what frustrations problems are worth solving? The answer many times involve listening and watching the process and people. See what frustrates them, wastes their time or money, or otherwise prevents them from completing a task they are trying to perform. Listen and see what a pain point for other people is.

By the end of this book, I would like to explore with you how to turn frustration into an opportunity for improvement, how apply Lean Manufacturing techniques to get rid of frustrations, become a superstar within your team and be highly valued for your contributions. Let's dive in and discover the power of frustration.

PART I: Potential of Frustration

―――

FRUSTRATION IS A FEELING we have all experienced at some point in our lives. It can arise from a variety of sources such as a lack of understanding, inconvenience, or unmet expectations.

However, frustration can also be an opportunity for improvement. It provides us with valuable feedback that we can use to identify areas of weakness and make necessary changes to improve the customer experience.

In this part of the book, we will explore the potential of frustration and how it can be leveraged to improve business operations.

We will begin by defining frustration and exploring its impact on the customer experience. In Part II, we will then discuss the importance of identifying and addressing customer frustrations, and the role of Lean Manufacturing in this process.

Chapter 1: The Nature of Frustration

"To conquer frustration, one must remain intensely focused on the outcome, not the obstacles." - T.F. Hodge

THE WAY THAT FRUSTRATION can manifest and impact in different situations depends on the eye of the beholder.

As Richard Branson once famously said, "There is no point in starting your own business unless you do it out of a sense of frustration. Great businesses aren't just about generating a return, they're about resolving problems that we can all identify with." (Capital, fifocapital.co.nz)

Frustration is a part of life, but how we deal with it can make all the difference. In this chapter, we will explore how frustration can manifest and impact us in different situations, and how we can focus on the outcome to overcome obstacles and achieve success.

Definition of Frustration

ACCORDING TO THE OXFORD Dictionary (Press, 2021), frustration is "the feeling of being upset or annoyed, especially because of inability to change or achieve something." It can also refer to "a source of annoyance or irritation."

Frustration is a feeling of disappointment or dissatisfaction that occurs when a customer's expectations are not met. It is a negative emotion that can be triggered by a variety of factors, including poor customer service, product defects, and long wait times.

Frustration can lead to a loss of trust and loyalty in a brand, and ultimately impact the bottom line of a business.

Frustration is a complex emotion that can result from a wide range of circumstances. It can occur when customers encounter unexpected barriers, such as confusing websites or long wait times, or when products fail to meet their expectations. Customers can become frustrated when they feel ignored, disrespected, or mistreated by a business, such as when they receive poor customer service.

Frustration can also arise from the feeling of helplessness when customers are unable to solve their problems or achieve their goals, even with the help of a business or customer service representative. This can cause them to feel a sense of powerlessness, leading to a negative emotional response.

It is important to understand that customers may experience frustration at any stage of their interaction with a business, from initial contact to post-purchase. As such, your businesses and team must take proactive measures to minimize the likelihood of frustrating experiences, and to respond effectively when they do occur.

The Psychology of Frustration

CUSTOMERS AND COMPANIES are both affected by frustration. Customers may experience negative word-of-mouth evaluations, decreased happiness, and a decreased chance of making future transactions as a result. Customer complaints and returns can result in decreased revenue, a clouded image, and higher expenses for companies.

Unmet expectations, perceived injustices, a lack of control, and trouble reaching objectives can all contribute to frustration. When your customers or team are unable to accomplish their goals, they may become frustrated, which can lead to negative feelings such as rage, regret, and sadness.

Frustration can have far-reaching consequences for both your client and your company. Customers who are frustrated may become unhappy with your product or service.

On the other hand, frustration can also have a negative impact on business operations. Employees who are frustrated with their work environment or lack of resources may become disengaged and less productive. This can lead to decreased efficiency, lower morale, and increased turnover.

To manage frustration effectively, it is important to understand its root causes and address them proactively. Companies can use customer feedback and data analysis to identify areas of frustration and make necessary improvements to their products or services. Additionally, providing employees with resources and support can help to reduce frustration and improve their job satisfaction.

Understanding the psychological processes underlying anger is crucial for managing it. For instance, if consumers feel out of control of the circumstance, they may be more likely to become frustrated. Companies can help to lessen consumer angst and boost satisfaction by giving them alternatives and letting them make decisions.

Customer Frustration and Satisfaction

THE PSYCHOLOGY OF FRUSTRATION is complex, and understanding it is key to improving customer satisfaction and loyalty. Frustration is often caused by a discrepancy between a customer's expectations and the actual experience.

However, it is not the initial problem that causes frustration, but rather how the problem is handled. A customer who feels heard, understood, and valued is more likely to remain loyal to a brand, even after a frustrating experience.

Customers who are frustrated are frequently searching for recognition and closure. If their dissatisfaction is not addressed effectively, it can lead to negative feelings such as anger, sadness, and even resentment towards the company. Customers' loyalty and support can increase when they believe their concerns are being handled.

Businesses or customer facing representatives should concentrate on active listening and empathy to effectively resolve customer frustration. This entails paying attention to the customer's emotions and worries while also taking prompt, courteous action to resolve their situation. It is crucial to communicate in a straightforward and open manner, including updates and status updates as required.

In addition to addressing the specific issue at hand, companies can also take steps to prevent future frustrations. This may involve improving processes or training employees to better handle customer concerns. By taking a proactive approach to addressing customer frustration, companies can improve the overall customer experience and build long-term loyalty.

Frustration and customer happiness are closely related, so it's important to track and gauge both indicators. Companies can effectively resolve areas of vulnerability and enhance the overall customer experience by knowing the variables that affect customer happiness.

To measure customer satisfaction, companies can use a variety of tools such as surveys, focus groups, and customer feedback. It is important to track satisfaction over time and identify trends and patterns. This information can be used to inform decision-making and drive continuous improvement.

Nowadays, there are more and more sources of frustrations, that ask you to stay ahead of the competition. These are some examples:

- **Changing Customer Needs and Preferences:** Customer needs and preferences are constantly changing, and companies must adapt to stay relevant.
- **Technological Advancements:** Technology is rapidly evolving, and companies that don't keep up with the latest trends risk falling behind.
- **Competition:** Competition is intense, and companies must continuously improve and innovate to stay ahead of their rivals.
- **New Market Entrants:** New players are always entering the market, giving much better service, and eating market share.

Chapter Summary/Key Takeaways

- Understanding the nature of frustration and its impact on customers and businesses is crucial for improving the customer experience.
- By recognising the psychology of frustration and responding appropriately, businesses can turn a negative experience into a positive one and build long-lasting customer loyalty.
- By proactively addressing areas of frustration and providing resources and support, companies can increase customer satisfaction, improve employee morale, and ultimately drive business success.

Chapter 2: From Frustration to Delight: Transforming Customer Experience

———

"Explain your anger instead of expressing it, and you'll find solutions instead of arguments." – Anonymous

TO GIVE VALUE TO CUSTOMERS, it is critical for businesses to understand the significance of a customer-centric approach. As many businesses have experienced, customer loyalty and happiness are essential to every business success in today's competitive industry.

Businesses that concentrate on the requirements and preferences of their clients are more likely to forge enduring bonds, boost sales, and keep a competitive edge.

Many studies have shown that when customers experience frustration with a product or service, their satisfaction and loyalty can be negatively impacted. On the other hand, businesses that actively seek out and address sources of frustration for their customers are more likely to see increased customer satisfaction, loyalty, and retention.

This chapter will cover the need to adopt a customer-centric mindset, the advantages it can have for your company, and the necessity of constant innovation and improvement to stay competitive.

The Power of Frustration as a Driver for Business Success

To address frustration and create a customer-centric approach in your business, it's important to listen to customer feedback and actively seek out sources of frustration. This can be done through customer surveys, user testing, and other feedback mechanisms.

Once sources of frustration have been identified, you can work to address them through process improvements, product development, or other means.

A customer-centric approach means that the customer is at the centre of everything a business does. It involves putting the customer's needs and wants first, understanding their preferences, and providing products and services that meet or exceed their expectations.

Here are some reasons why a using frustration as a driver is essential to your business success:

- **Builds Trust and Loyalty:** Customers are more likely to trust and remain loyal to companies that show they care about their needs and preferences.
- **Improves Customer Satisfaction:** By focusing on what customers want and need, businesses can improve their overall satisfaction with the products and services they receive.
- **Increases Revenue:** Satisfied customers are more likely to make repeat purchases and recommend the company to others, which can help increase revenue.
- **Improves Brand Reputation:** A customer-centric approach can help build a positive reputation for the brand, which can attract new customers and increase market share.

- **Competitive Advantage:** Companies that focus on the customer's needs and preferences are more likely to stand out from their competitors and gain a competitive advantage.
- **Increased Customer Lifetime Value:** Satisfied customers are more likely to make repeat purchases and become long-term customers, which can increase their lifetime value.
- **Higher Customer Retention:** A customer-centric approach can help reduce customer churn rates and improve customer

retention, which can save money on customer acquisition costs.

- **Better Product Development:** By understanding customer needs and preferences, companies can develop better products and services that meet their customers' expectations.

While a customer-centric approach is essential, it's not enough to maintain a competitive edge in today's marketplace. Companies must also focus on continuous improvement and innovation to stay ahead of the competition.

Understanding the customer journey and identifying pain points

TO PROVIDE A TRULY customer-centric experience, it is important for businesses to understand the customer journey and identify pain points along the way. By doing so, companies can improve the overall customer experience and increase customer satisfaction.

The customer journey is the path that a customer takes from the initial awareness of a product or service to the final purchase and beyond. Understanding and mapping the customer journey is essential for creating a positive customer experience. In this chapter, we'll explore the steps to building a customer journey and identifying pain points.

A great definition to this process is the one mentioned by Gene Cornfield in his article Designing Customer Journeys for the Post-Pandemic World, (Cornfield, 2021) "Influence can be more effective when journeys and experiences are customer-centric, designed not as a path to purchase, but as a path to purpose."

The standard process to create a customer journey involves:

Step 1 - Define Your Customer Personas: The first step in building a customer journey is to define your customer personas. Customer personas are fictional representations of your ideal customers, and they help you understand their needs, wants, and behaviours. To create customer personas, you can use demographic information, customer feedback, and other data sources.

Step 2 - Map the Customer Journey: Once you have defined your customer personas, the next step is to map the customer journey. Mapping the customer journey involves identifying each step of the customer's experience, from the initial awareness of your product or service to the post-purchase follow-up. This step requires a deep understanding of your customer personas and their behaviours.

Step 3 - Identify Pain Points: The next step in building a customer journey is to identify pain points. Pain points are the areas of the customer journey where customers experience frustration, confusion, or dissatisfaction. To identify pain points, you can use customer feedback, user testing, and other research methods. It's essential to prioritise pain points based on their impact on the customer experience and your business objectives.

Step 4 - Develop Solutions: Once pain points have been identified, the next step is to develop solutions to address them. This can involve process improvements, product changes, or other means. It's essential to prioritize solutions based on their impact on the customer experience and business objectives.

Step 5 - Test and Iterate: The final step in building a customer journey is to test and iterate. Testing involves implementing solutions and measuring their impact on the customer experience. Iteration involves adjusting based on the results of testing. This step is essential for continuous improvement and ensuring that the customer journey addresses your customer purpose effectively.

Strategies for addressing customer frustrations and turning them into delight

CUSTOMER FRUSTRATIONS are inevitable in any business, but it's how a business responds to these frustrations that can make all the difference. In this section, let's explore strategies for addressing customer frustrations and turning them into delight.

According to Qualtrics XM Institute, "Only one in five consumers will forgive a bad experience at a company whose customer service they rate as "very poor." (Nearly 80% will forgive a bad experience if they rate the service team as "very good.")" (Dorsey, Segall, & Temkin)

When a customer experiences a problem or frustration, the first step in turning it into delight is to acknowledge the issue. This can be as simple as saying "I'm sorry to hear that you're experiencing this problem" or "I understand how frustrating this can be." Acknowledging the issue shows that the business is listening to the customer and taking their concerns seriously.

Once the issue has been acknowledged, the next step is to offer a solution. This can be anything from offering a refund or exchange to providing additional support or assistance. It's important to offer a solution that addresses the customer's specific issue and shows that the business is committed to resolving the problem.

Going above and beyond to address a customer's frustration can turn a negative experience into a positive one. This can include offering a personalised solution or a special discount, providing additional support or resources, or simply taking the time to listen to the customer's concerns. Going above and beyond shows that the business is willing to go the extra mile to ensure customer satisfaction.

Following up with the customer after their issue has been resolved is a key strategy for turning frustration into delight. This can be as simple as sending a follow-up email or making a phone call to ensure that the customer is satisfied with the solution. Following up shows that the business values the customer's feedback and is committed to providing excellent customer service.

Addressing customer frustrations and turning them into delight is essential for building customer loyalty and increasing customer satisfaction. By acknowledging the frustration, offering a solution, going above and beyond, and following up, your team and businesses can show their commitment to providing excellent customer service and turn negative experiences into positive ones.

Chapter Summary/Key Takeaways

- A customer-centric strategy is crucial for any company that wishes to thrive in the modern marketplace. Businesses may boost income and trust by prioritising their customers.
- To keep one step ahead of your competition and maintain relevance in a market that is changing quickly, continuous improvement and innovation are also essential.
- By placing an equal emphasis on continual innovation and improvement as well as customer centricity, your team and business may grow sales and maintain a competitive advantage.

PART II: Finding What is Worth Solving

WHILE FRUSTRATION CAN provide valuable opportunities for improvement, not all frustrations are created equal. To make the most of these opportunities, it is important to identify the frustrations that have the greatest impact on customer satisfaction, loyalty, and business success.

Finding frustrations worth solving requires a deep understanding of customer needs, pain points, and behaviours. It also involves a systematic approach to gathering and analysing data, as well as a willingness to experiment and iterate on potential solutions.

This section of the book will cover a variety of topics related to finding frustrations worth solving, including different methods of gathering customer feedback, such as surveys, focus groups, and interviews. We will also discuss how to use this feedback to identify common frustrations and pain points.

We will explore different types of customer data, such as purchase history, website interactions, and social media engagement. We will also discuss how to use this data to identify trends and patterns.

Not all frustrations are equally important to address. We will discuss how to prioritize frustrations based on factors such as customer impact, business impact, and feasibility.

Once potential frustrations have been identified and prioritized, it is time to start ideating and testing solutions. We will explore different methods of ideation, such as brainstorming and design thinking. We will also discuss how to test and iterate on potential solutions to find the most effective ones.

By the end of Part II, you will have a good understanding of how to identify and prioritize frustrations worth solving, and how to develop and test potential solutions. This knowledge will be essential for improving customer satisfaction, loyalty, and business success.

Chapter 3: Finding Frustrations Worth Solving

"Frustration is the fuel that can lead to the development of an innovative and useful idea." – Marley Dias

ELIMINATING FRUSTRATIONS requires first identifying and prioritising the most significant frustrations that are worth solving. But how do you determine which frustrations to tackle first?

In this chapter, we will explore several tools that can be used to identify frustrations worth solving, including customer feedback analysis, surveys, focus groups, observation, and other tools.

Tools for Finding Frustrations Worth Solving

TO MEASURE CUSTOMER experience, you can use a variety of tools such as surveys, focus groups, and customer feedback. Some of the most frequent tools used are:

- **Customer Feedback:** Getting and analysing customer feedback can be done from various sources like social media platforms, online reviews, and customer service inquiries. All can help you identify patterns in the types of frustrations that customers experience. Currently Sentiment analysis tools using Artificial Intelligence can be used to automate this process, allowing you to identify trends quickly and easily in customer feedback.
- **Surveys**: Surveys are a great way to gather information from many customers. Using online survey tools, you can gather feedback on specific products or services, or gather

information on broader market trends. By analysing the results of surveys, you can identify which frustrations are most common among customers.

- **Focus Groups:** Focus groups are a great way to gather in-depth feedback from a small group of customers. Depending on your situation it may not be the best option, due to the influence between participants. However still a valid tool where participants can discuss their frustrations in detail, providing valuable insights into the root causes of the frustrations. With video conferencing tools focus groups can also be conducted remotely, making it easier to gather feedback from a geographically diverse customer base.
- **Observation**: Observing customers as they use your product or service. This can help you identify areas where customers become frustrated or confused. You can use tools like heat mapping software for example, to analyse how customers interact with your website or simply sitting on the bench in front of your store to see how customers interact with your staff and products. This can help you identify specific areas for improvement, such as confusing navigation or difficult-to-find information.
- **Customer Journey Mapping**: Mapping out the customer journey can help you identify areas where customers may be experiencing frustration. This process involves creating a visual representation of the customer's interactions with the company at each touchpoint. can be used to create detailed customer journey maps, helping to identify the areas where customers are most likely to become frustrated.

The Importance of Identifying and Prioritising Customer Frustrations

CONSIDERING THAT NOT all frustrations are equally important to address, it is important to listen to customer feedback and gather data on their experiences.

This may involve conducting surveys, analysing social media mentions, or tracking customer interactions on a website or app. By gathering this information, you can gain insights into the specific pain points and frustrations that customers are experiencing, then can prioritise frustrations based on factors such as customer impact, business impact, and feasibility.

As Simon Sinek mentions in his great book Find your Why (Sinek), "When you find yourself in a situation where you're frustrated—it "just doesn't feel right" yet you "can't put your finger on it"—use your HOWs to see if you can find out what's out of alignment. Sometimes by simply running down the list of HOWs, you'll immediately be able to put into words what isn't working for you. Once you can put your frustration into words, it makes it easier to ask for what you need to get things back on track."

Prioritising frustrations based on factors such as customer impact, business impact, and feasibility are one way of identifying the importance of what you need to address first, while allocate your resources for maximum impact.

Some standard steps that you can use to prioritise customer frustrations include:

1. **Identify and list all the customer frustrations known:** This can be done through customer feedback, data analysis, or customer service interactions.

2. **Assess the customer impact (High to Low):** Evaluate the level of impact each frustration has on customer satisfaction and loyalty. Ask questions such as: How frequently do customers experience this frustration? How severe is the impact on their experience with the product or service? How likely are they to stop doing business with the company because of this frustration?

3. **Evaluate the business impact (High to Low):** Consider the potential financial impact of addressing each frustration. Ask questions such as: How much revenue is being lost due to this frustration? How much will be addressing this frustration increase revenue or decrease costs?

4. **Determine the feasibility (High to Low):** Evaluate the practicality of addressing each frustration. Consider factors such as time, resources, and technical capabilities. Ask questions such as: How much time and resources will it take to address this frustration? Is the company capable of addressing this frustration with its current technology or infrastructure?

5. **Prioritise the frustrations:** Once all the customer frustrations have been assessed based on the above factors, prioritise them based on their level of impact on customer satisfaction and loyalty, potential financial impact, and feasibility. Focus on addressing the frustrations with the highest priority first.

Here is an example that you can use as a guide for your specific situation (if you prefer can convert it into a simple scoring table):

- Frustration: Long wait times on customer support calls
  - Customer Impact: High
  - Business Impact: High
  - Feasibility: Moderate
  - Priority: 1
- Frustration: Limited product features compared to

competitors
- ○ Customer Impact: High
- ○ Business Impact: Moderate
- ○ Feasibility: Moderate
- ○ Priority: 2
- Frustration: Inconsistent product quality
  - ○ Customer Impact: High
  - ○ Business Impact: Moderate
  - ○ Feasibility: Low
  - ○ Priority: 3
- Frustration: Poor communication regarding product updates
  - ○ Customer Impact: Medium
  - ○ Business Impact: Low
  - ○ Feasibility: High
  - ○ Priority: 4

By following these steps, you can focus your company and team on addressing the most impactful customer frustrations, maximizing the impact of their improvement efforts, and ultimately improving customer satisfaction, loyalty, and business success.

Method for analysing customer feedback

ANALYSING CUSTOMER data can identify pain points and areas for improvement. By doing so, you can gain valuable insights into what frustrates their customers and work to develop solutions that meet their needs.

Getting as much data as you can on customer preferences, demands, and pain spots is the aim. With the use of this information, you may gain a deeper insight of your clients' wants and needs, empowering you to produce better products and provide better marketing and customer service. In the long run, this may result in higher client retention, satisfaction, and profitability.

Some of the methods normally used to analyse customer data that you can use include:

1. The first step in data analysis is to identify the sources of data. This could include customer feedback from surveys, reviews, social media comments, customer service calls, or any other customer touchpoints.
2. Once the data sources are identified, it's important to define the problem to be solved. For example, the problem could be long wait times on customer service calls.
3. Data cleaning involves removing any irrelevant or duplicate data and organizing it in a way that can be easily analysed. This step is crucial for ensuring that the data is accurate and reliable.
4. Once the data is clean and organized, it's time to analyse it. Various data analysis techniques can be used, such as statistical analysis, sentiment analysis, or text mining. For example, statistical analysis could be used to identify the most common reasons for long wait times on customer service calls.
5. After analysing the data, it's important to interpret the results to gain valuable insights. For example, the data analysis may reveal that most long wait times are due to a lack of available customer service representatives during peak hours.
6. Based on the insights gained from the data analysis, you can start developing solutions to address the identified problem. For example, a company could hire additional customer service representatives during peak hours to reduce wait times.
7. After a solution has been implemented, it's important to monitor and measure its success. This can be done by collecting additional data and comparing it to the pre-implementation data. For example, a company could track wait times on

customer service calls before and after the implementation of additional customer service representatives.

By following these steps for data analysis, you can gain valuable insights into customer frustrations and develop effective solutions to address them.

Chapter Summary/Key Takeaways

- Identifying and prioritising frustrations to reduce or eliminate is essential for improving the customer experience.
- By using tools like customer feedback analysis, surveys, focus groups, observation, and tools like sentiment analysis, companies can gain valuable insights into the frustrations that customers face.

THIS CAN HELP PRIORITISE which frustrations to tackle first, ultimately leading to a better overall customer experience.

Chapter 4: Frustration Means Improvement Opportunity

———

"You're frustrated because you keep waiting for the blooming of flowers of which you have yet to sow the seeds." — *Steve Maraboli*

FRUSTRATION IS A NATURAL reaction to encountering obstacles or inefficiencies in a process. However, in the world of innovation, frustration is viewed as an opportunity for improvement.

By identifying and addressing the sources of frustration, you can streamline processes, improve customer experiences, and increase overall efficiency.

Managing frustration can lead to creative problem-solving, innovative thinking, and ultimately, better outcomes for both your business and customers.

By the application of Lean Manufacturing principles, you may encourage your team to learn and implement problem-solving strategies by viewing frustration as a chance for improvement.

An excellent approach to problem-solving tries to reach three goals: enhancing customer experience, continuously refining processes and constantly helping your team for better understand their and one another roles.

In this chapter, we will explore several tools borrowed from the Lean Manufacturing philosophy that you can use to reduce frustrations and continuously improve in the customer journey.

Introduction to Lean Manufacturing Principles

LEAN MANUFACTURING philosophy started to give only value to the customers, hence anything that is not value added is not helping the purpose.

According to the lean philosophy, "Value" is any action or process that the customer pays for or is willing to pay for.

One of the most suitable definitions of Lean for the objectives of this book is by Mr. John Shook, who said that "Lean is a philosophy which shortens the time between the customer order and the product build/ shipment by eliminating sources of waste."

Lean Manufacturing is a systematic approach to identifying and eliminating waste in a production process. Lean tools are used to streamline processes, reduce lead times, and improve quality. In this chapter, we will discuss some of the most used lean tools, including Kaizen, 8D, A3, VSM, and DMAIC. We will explore how these tools can be applied to eliminate market frustrations and improve the overall customer experience.

As discussed in my previous book, "Sorry About the Wait - a lean guide to reducing wait times and improve customer experience" (Estrada, 2023), implementing lean methodologies can help you reduce waste and improve customer experience.

Continuous improvement - Kaizen

KAIZEN IS A JAPANESE term that means "continuous improvement." It is a philosophy that encourages small, incremental improvements in processes over time. One example of Kaizen in action is the use of daily activities to keep a workspace organized and efficient. By eliminating clutter and creating a standard for cleanliness and organization, employees can work more efficiently and effectively, which ultimately leads to improved customer satisfaction.

Although some Kaizen or improvements can be analysed and implemented quickly, there are other situation where you need more time and analysing before improving.

The standard steps to implement an improvement can be based in the continuous improvement Plan-Do-Check-Act (PDCA) cycle. This cycle involves four stages: planning, executing, checking, and acting.

It is a very efficient approach to problem-solving that can enable you and your team to identify issues, develop solutions, implement them, and monitor their effectiveness.

The steps that you can use are:

Plan

1. Defining the problem or opportunity for improvement. Defining the Team.
2. Gathering data to understand the current process or system.
3. Brainstorming and analysing the current information or data.

Do

1. Developing and implementing the proposed solutions to address the identified issues.

Check

1. Evaluating the effectiveness of the solutions and adjusting as needed.

Act

1. Standardising the improved process or system either in a work instruction or visual guide, to ensure continuous improvement over time.

Eight Disciplines - 8D

8D IS A PROBLEM-SOLVING methodology that is used to identify, correct, and prevent problems.

One example of using 8D to eliminate market frustrations is when a customer reports a problem with a product. By following the 8D process, the company can quickly identify the root cause of the problem and take corrective action to prevent it from happening in the future.

Here are the eight steps involved in the 8D process:

D1 - Establish the Team: Identify the team of people who will be responsible for addressing the problem and assign roles and responsibilities.

D2 - Describe the Problem: Clearly define the problem, its impact, and its location. Gather data on the problem, and collect customer complaints or feedback, if available.

D3 - Contain the Problem: Implement immediate actions to prevent the problem from getting worse. Identify any temporary solutions or workarounds that can be implemented to mitigate the impact of the problem.

D4 - Identify the Root Cause: Analyse the data collected in step two to identify the root cause of the problem. Use tools such as the 5 Whys or fishbone diagrams to uncover the underlying causes of the problem.

D5 - Develop and Verify Solutions: Develop and select solutions to address the root cause of the problem. Test the proposed solutions to ensure they will effectively resolve the problem.

D6 - Implement Permanent Corrective Actions: Implement the solutions identified in step five. Ensure that all relevant stakeholders are aware of the changes and that they have been effectively implemented.

D7 - Prevent Recurrence: Verify that the problem has been resolved and that it is unlikely to recur. Implement additional measures to prevent the problem from recurring in the future.

D8 - Recognise the Team: Recognise the contributions of the team and celebrate their success in addressing the problem. Document the entire process for future reference and continuous improvement.

Problem Solving - A3

A3 IS ONE OF MY FAVOURITE problem-solving techniques, because it uses a single sheet of paper to document the problem, the current state, the desired state, and the action plan to get there.

The A3 methodology is very similar to the 8D, the main difference is that all fits normally in one piece of paper, it is designed to encourage cross-functional collaboration and visual communication.

One example of using A3 to eliminate market frustrations is when a company wants to improve the customer experience at a retail store. By using the A3 process to identify the current state, desired state, and action plan, the company can create a clear roadmap for improving the store layout, customer service, and product selection.

The A3 report typically includes the following elements:

1. **Background**: A summary of the problem, including its history and any relevant context.
2. **Current Situation**: A detailed description of the current situation, including data and facts about the problem.
3. **Analysis**: A root cause analysis that identifies the underlying cause(s) of the problem.
4. **Countermeasures**: A list of proposed solutions to address the root cause(s) of the problem.
5. **Implementation Plan**: A plan for implementing the proposed solutions, including timelines and responsibilities.
6. **Follow-up:** A plan for monitoring progress and verifying that the problem has been fully resolved.

Value Stream Mapping - VSM

VSM STANDS FOR Value Stream Mapping and is a tool used to visualize the flow of materials and information through a production process. VSM is designed to identify waste and inefficiencies in the process and highlight areas for improvement.

One example of using VSM to eliminate market frustrations is when a company wants to reduce the lead time for delivering a product to a customer. By mapping out the value stream and identifying areas of waste, your company can streamline any process, reduce lead times, and ultimately improve the customer experience.

By mapping out each step of the journey, organisations can identify areas where they can improve the customer experience.

The standard process to do a value stream map include:

1. **Choose a process to map:** Identify the process that you want

to map and improve. It could be a specific area of your business, such as production or customer service.

2. **Assemble a team:** Select a team of individuals who are familiar with the process and have the expertise in your process. The team could include managers, supervisors, and front-line employees.

3. **Collect data:** Gather data on the process being mapped, including cycle times, lead times, inventory levels, and other relevant metrics.

4. **Draw a current state map:** Create a visual representation of the current process, including the flow of materials and information, process steps, and any bottlenecks or waste. This is typically done using a flowchart or process map.

5. **Identify areas of waste:** Analyse the current state map to identify areas of waste, such as excess inventory, overproduction, and waiting time.

6. **Develop a future state map:** Based on the analysis of the current state map, create a visual representation of the ideal process, including changes to eliminate waste and improve flow.

7. **Implement improvements:** Use the future state map as a guide to implement improvements to the process. This may involve changes to layout, equipment, or procedures.

8. **Monitor progress:** Track the process over time to measure progress and identify further opportunities for improvement.

DMAIC

DMAIC STANDS FOR DEFINE, Measure, Analyse, Improve, and Control. It is a problem-solving methodology that is used to improve a process by identifying and eliminating defects.

DMAIC is typically used in Six Sigma, a data-driven approach to quality improvement. One example of using DMAIC to eliminate market frustrations is when a company wants to improve the quality of a product. By defining the problem, measuring the current state, analysing the root cause of defects, implementing improvements, and controlling the process, the company can improve the quality of the product and eliminate frustrations for customers.

Voice of Customer - VoC

THE VOICE OF CUSTOMER (VoC) is a key component of lean methodologies and can be used to reduce frustration and is usually used during a specific improvement project.

In the Lean Philosophy the term "Customer" addresses the External and Internal customers, hence depending on the context or improvement you need to keep the definition clear. As an example, if you are reducing frustration in an internal matter with employees in an organization, you could call it the Voice of Employee as well.

The VoC is a process of capturing and analysing customer feedback and insights to understand their needs and preferences. By doing so, teams and businesses can make informed decisions and take action to improve the customer experience.

The usual steps include:

1. Capturing the VoC is to identify the different touchpoints in the customer journey where feedback can be collected. This can include surveys, interviews, focus groups, social media monitoring, and other methods. It's important to choose the right method for the specific touchpoint and to make it easy and convenient for the customer to provide feedback.
2. Once the feedback is collected, it's important to analyse and

categorize it to identify patterns and trends. This can be done through data analysis or by using tools such as affinity diagrams or journey mapping. The goal is to understand the customer's pain points, preferences, and expectations.

3. The next step is to prioritize, and act based on the feedback received. This can include making process improvements, changing products or services, or implementing new initiatives. By acting on the feedback received, you can demonstrate to your customers how you are listening and taking their needs seriously.

4. Finally, it's important to communicate the results of the VoC process to all stakeholders, including employees, customers, and leadership. This can include sharing success stories, improvements made, and plans for future initiatives. By doing so, organizations can build trust and credibility with their customers and demonstrate their commitment to delivering exceptional customer experiences.

VoC is a crucial part of lean approaches and can be utilised to lessen annoyance for both the organisation and the client. Organizations may enhance the customer experience and ultimately promote corporate success by collecting, analysing, and acting on customer feedback.

Design Thinking

DESIGN THINKING IS a human-centered approach to problem-solving that is becoming increasingly popular in various industries. The methodology emphasizes empathy and understanding the needs and frustrations of users to create solutions that truly meet their needs.

By focusing on the user experience and identifying pain points, Design Thinking can help reduce customer frustration and improve overall satisfaction.

To get started with this methodology, here are the main basic steps:

1. **Empathise:** Understanding the user's needs, thoughts, and feelings.
2. **Define:** Clearly defining the problem and focusing on the user's pain points.
3. **Ideate:** Generating creative ideas and potential solutions.
4. **Prototype:** Creating low-fidelity prototypes to test ideas and gather feedback.
5. **Test:** Gathering feedback from users to refine the solution and improve the user experience.
6. **Implement:** Finalising the solution and implementing it into the user's journey.

It's worth noting that design thinking is an iterative process, and it's common for designers to cycle through these steps multiple times to refine and improve the solution.

Defining Roles and Responsibilities to Reduce Frustration

A BIG SOURCE OF FRUSTRATION, especially from an internal team is about what roles they play and where their responsibilities lie. Defining roles and responsibilities is critical to reducing frustration in any organization. When employees are unclear about their responsibilities or feel that their role is ill-defined, they can become frustrated, leading to decreased motivation and productivity. This, in turn, can have a negative impact on the customer experience.

It's critical to clearly define roles and duties and properly convey them to all team members to prevent frustration. As part of this, it is important to specify the duties and expectations of each team member as well as their amount of authority and power to make decisions. Everyone on the team is more likely to be engaged, motivated, and focused on providing outstanding customer experiences when they are aware of their responsibilities and how they contribute to the overall success of the company.

One effective way to define roles and responsibilities is using job descriptions. A well-written job description should include a summary of the role, a list of key responsibilities and duties, required qualifications, and any other relevant information. This document can be used as a reference for employees to understand their job expectations and can be helpful in setting performance goals and expectations.

Another important tool is the creation of an organizational chart. This chart should clearly outline the reporting structure, who is responsible for what areas of the business, and how decisions are made. This chart can be used to ensure that all team members understand the chain of command and who they should go to for specific questions or concerns.

Finally, it's important to have ongoing communication and training to ensure that roles and responsibilities are understood and being followed. This includes regular check-ins, team meetings, and training sessions to reinforce expectations and address any issues or concerns.

By taking the time to define roles and responsibilities clearly, you can reduce frustration, increase productivity, and ultimately deliver a better customer experience.

Chapter Summary/Key Takeaways

- The tested Lean Manufacturing tools are powerful techniques for eliminating customer frustrations, improving quality, and ultimately improving the customer experience.
- By using these tools, your team and company can streamline processes, reduce lead times, and identify and eliminate defects. By doing so, they can eliminate market frustrations and improve customer satisfaction.
- Voice of Customer - VoC is a critical component of lean methodologies and can be used to reduce frustration for both the customer and the organization.
- Define roles and responsibilities clearly, so you can reduce frustration in your Team, increase productivity, and ultimately deliver a better customer experience.

PART III: Leveraging Technologies to Achieve Success

———

BY APPLYING LEAN MANUFACTURING principles, you can encourage your team to learn and implement problem-solving strategies by viewing frustration as an opportunity for progress.

However, to truly eliminate customer and business frustrations, you need to leverage the power of technology. In this part of the book, we will explore various of the current technologies that can help you identify and eliminate sources of frustration in your processes and systems.

From customer feedback tools to process automation software, there is an always evolving range of technologies that can help you streamline your operations, reduce waste, and improve customer satisfaction.

We will also discuss the current technologies available for your business and how to effectively implement them. My goal by the end of this section of the book is to look at some examples and applications of technology that can help you eliminate frustrations and improve your business processes.

Chapter 5: Technologies for Eliminating Frustrations

───

"Frustration is a very positive sign. It means that the solution to your problem is within range, but what you're currently doing isn't working, and you need to change your approach to achieve your goal." – Anthony Robbins

ADVANCEMENTS IN TECHNOLOGY have enabled companies to enhance the customer experience and eliminate market frustrations in ways that were previously impossible. In this chapter, we will explore several technologies that can be used to eliminate frustration in customers and business, including chatbots, artificial intelligence (AI), augmented reality (AR), and mobile applications.

In the current digital era, technology has completely changed how businesses function and interact with their customers. Using the right technologies is critical to your success and the customer experience. Because technological advancement has created new opportunities and challenges for businesses, it is also critical to ensure that the technologies align with your business goals and customer needs.

By leveraging the right technologies, you can streamline your operations, improve efficiency, and deliver exceptional customer experiences. From automation tools to artificial intelligence and machine learning, there are various technologies available that can help businesses in different ways.

In this part, we'll explore how you can leverage some technologies to achieve success and eliminate customer and business frustrations.

Overview of Technology Trends

THE WORLD OF TECHNOLOGY is constantly evolving, and with it, the ways in which businesses interact with their customers. The number of ways that organisations can improve their operations and improve the customer experience has increased because of technological improvements.

It is amazing how technology is always changing, and with it the customers experience, so is important to follow technological developments that are significantly affecting how frustrated customers are handled and how well businesses work.

One of the most important technology trends for businesses to pay attention to is the rise of artificial intelligence (AI). AI is becoming increasingly popular in customer service operations, with many businesses implementing chatbots and other AI-powered tools to automate customer interactions. This not only provides customers with more immediate assistance but also frees up customer service representatives to focus on more complex issues.

Another key technology trend that many of us use nowadays is the Internet of Things (IoT), which refers to the network of physical devices, vehicles, home appliances, and other items embedded with sensors, software, and network connectivity. This technology has the potential to significantly enhance the customer experience by allowing businesses to use data to constantly improve how customers are using products and services. This data can then be used to identify pain points and areas for improvement, leading to a more seamless customer experience.

Finally, the use of cloud technology is also becoming increasingly important in reducing customer frustrations and improving business operations. Cloud technology allows businesses to store and access data remotely, which means that employees can access important information from anywhere and at any time. This can lead to more efficient operations and better customer service, as employees can quickly access the information, they need to resolve customer issues.

Overall, these technological advancements can provide your businesses with a powerful toolset to reduce customer frustrations and improve your operations.

Examples of Applicable Technologies to Reduce Frustration

EXAMPLES OF EMERGING technologies for reducing frustration and improving business outcomes are constantly emerging, so this section will only highlight some of the current tools that have the potential to improve customer experience.

Technologies can provide you with valuable insights into customer behaviour, as well as enabling businesses to automate certain processes and improve operational efficiency.

As these technologies continue to evolve, it is likely that they will play an increasingly important role in helping you to reduce frustration and improve customer experience and operational efficiency.

Some applicable examples of emerging technologies that can have great potential applications for reducing frustration and improving business are:

- **Chatbots:** Chatbots are computer programs that can simulate conversation with human users. By using natural language processing (NLP), chatbots can understand customer inquiries, interact with customers in real-time, answer their questions and provide helpful responses. Nowadays you can use chatbots to address customer concerns, reducing frustration and improving the overall customer experience quickly and efficiently. Some benefits for your business include 24/7 availability, quick response times, and reduced customer wait times.

- **Artificial Intelligence (AI)**: AI is a technology that allows machines to perform tasks that typically require human intelligence, such as recognizing speech, making decisions, and learning. You can use AI to analyse customer data, predict customer needs and automate repetitive tasks. Some benefits for your business include personalised customer experiences, improved customer service and reduced operational costs.

- **Augmented Reality (AR)**: AR is a technology that allows users to interact with digital information that is superimposed on the real world. Companies can use AR to provide customers with immersive experiences, customers can visualize products and services in real-world settings. Some benefits for your business include enhanced product visualization, improved customer engagement, and reduced product returns.

- **Mobile Applications**: Mobile applications can be used to provide customers with convenient access to products and services. Companies can use mobile apps to streamline customer interactions, reducing frustration and improving the overall customer experience. For example, some benefits for your business include allowing customers to place orders and pay for purchases directly from their phones, reducing wait times and increasing convenience.

- **Internet of Things (IoT)**: IoT technology can be used to collect data from connected devices and sensors, enabling businesses to monitor and optimise processes in real-time. Benefits include improved process efficiency, reduced downtime, and increased product quality.

- **Virtual Reality (VR)**: VR technology can be used to create immersive experiences that simulate real-world scenarios.

Benefits include improved customer engagement, enhanced product visualization, and reduced costs associated with physical prototypes, which allows customers to configure and interact with virtual models.

- **Robotic Process Automation (RPA):** RPA technology can be used to automate repetitive and manual tasks, improving staff with tasks such as data entry and processing, so they can focus on higher-value activities. Benefits include improved process efficiency, reduced errors, and cost savings.

Metrics for Measuring Impact

MEASURING THE EFFECTS of technology implementation and any frustration reduction initiatives is crucial for assessing the efficacy of your efforts and justifying the time and resources invested.

There are certain clear measures to track progress and success in frustration reduction projects. Customer satisfaction, efficiency, cost savings and your specific business metrics should all be linked to these metrics.

Using precise metrics will help you gauge customer loyalty and likely to promote your product or service to others, discover areas for improvement, track progress over time, and most importantly, compare against industry standards and competitors.

Metrics such as Net Promoter Score (NPS), Customer Satisfaction Score (CSAT), and Customer Effort Score (CES) can provide you with valuable insights into how customers perceive the improvements made to their experience.

A good practice is to track them over time to evaluate the effectiveness of frustration reduction initiatives.

Here some more details:

- **Net Promoter Score (NPS):** NPS is a measure of customer loyalty and satisfaction. It is calculated by asking customers to rate, on a scale of 0-10, how likely they are to recommend your company to a friend or colleague. The NPS calculation formula is: % of Promoters (customers who rate 9-10) - % of Detractors (customers who rate 0-6). A higher NPS indicates greater customer satisfaction and loyalty, which can lead to increased customer retention, referral business, and revenue.

- **Customer Effort Score (CES):** CES measures the ease with which customers can interact with a company and get their needs met. It is calculated by asking customers to rate, on a scale of 1-5, how easy it was to resolve their issue or complete their task. Calculation formula is the average score from the responses received on a scale of 1-5. There is no industry standard for calculating customer effort scores. However, depending on how your survey scales are organized, average effort scores that trend further towards either end of your scale indicate where your company is in terms of customer experience.

- **Customer Satisfaction Score (CSAT):** CSAT is a widely used metric for measuring how satisfied customers are with a particular product, service, or interaction. It is usually calculated by asking customers to rate their experience on a scale of 1 to 5 or 1 to 10, with higher scores indicating greater satisfaction. The formula for CSAT is Number of satisfied customers / Total number of survey responses x 100%. High CSAT scores can lead to increased customer loyalty, repeat business, and positive word-of-mouth recommendations.

- **Customer Churn Rate:** Churn rate measures the rate at which customers stop doing business with a company. It is calculated by dividing the number of customers lost during a certain period by the total number of customers at the beginning of that period. A lower churn rate indicates greater customer retention and loyalty, which can lead to increased revenue and profitability over time. By tracking churn rate, you can identify patterns and root causes of customer dissatisfaction and take proactive measures to address them. This metric can provide insights into the success of frustration reduction initiatives. By reducing customer frustration, businesses can increase customer loyalty and ultimately drive more revenue.

In addition to customer-focused metrics, you could also track business success metrics such as cost savings, productivity improvements, and efficiency gains. By reducing frustration and improving processes, you can save time and resources, which can ultimately lead to increased profitability.

Chapter Summary/Key Takeaways

- Advancements in technology can provide you with new and innovative ways to improve the customer experience and eliminate market frustrations.
- By using technologies such as chatbots, AI, AR, and mobile applications, you can streamline customer interactions, provide immersive experiences, and quickly address customer concerns.
- As technology continues to evolve, you would need to innovate and leverage new tools to provide the best possible experience for your customers.
- Establishing and tracking metrics for measuring the impact of frustration reduction initiatives is crucial for your business. Along with understanding the effectiveness of your efforts to continuously improve the customer experience.

Chapter 6: Examples of Frustration Elimination that Works

———

"Frustration is the first step toward improvement. It's only when I face frustration and use it to fuel my dedication that I feel myself moving forward." – John Bingham

IN THIS CHAPTER, WE will look at some hypothetical and real cases of successful examples of organisations that have effectively handled and removed consumer frustrations. We can learn from these examples some methods, techniques, and outcomes by examining them. We will investigate a wide range of industries and companies, from small startups to major multinationals.

Customer dissatisfaction is a universal issue, and companies that can effectively solve it have a huge competitive edge. These business examples show a strong awareness of their customers' needs and innovative solutions to minimise problems and improve customer experiences.

Whether it's streamlining processes, improving communication channels, or incorporating new technologies, the companies highlighted here have found unique ways to address customer frustrations and create more satisfying experiences.

By examining these examples, we can learn from their successes and apply their strategies to our own businesses. Let's look at these case studies and figure out how to get rid of frustration.

Hypothetical Case Study: Reducing Customer Frustration in a Healthcare Organization

BACKGROUND

A healthcare business has been facing challenges with customer frustration related to long wait times, lack of communication, and confusion regarding the appointment process. The business has identified these issues as critical areas for improvement to increase customer satisfaction and retention.

Step 1: Identifying the Problem using A3 Problem Solving

The healthcare business decides to use A3 problem solving to identify the root causes of customer frustration. After gathering feedback from customer surveys, the team identifies the lack of clear communication and lengthy wait times as the key issues. The team then identifies the underlying reasons for these problems, which include lack of staff training, inefficient scheduling processes, and limited resources.

Step 2: Implementing Lean Manufacturing Techniques

The healthcare business applies Lean Manufacturing principles such as Value Stream Mapping to address these issues. The team conducts staff training sessions to improve communication with customers, redesigns the scheduling process to reduce wait times, and allocates additional resources to the customer service department. These improvements help to eliminate bottlenecks and create a more efficient process for customers.

Step 3: Implementing Chatbot Technology

To further improve customer experience and reduce frustration, the healthcare business implements chatbot technology. This technology allows customers or patients to receive immediate assistance and answers to common questions without having to wait on hold or speak to a representative. The chatbot is programmed with a list of frequently asked questions and answers and is available 24/7 to assist customers.

Step 4: Measuring Customer Experience with Customer Effort Score (CES)

The healthcare business uses the Customer Effort Score (CES) to measure the success of the frustration elimination project. The CES measures how much effort customers need to put in to get their issues resolved. The business sends out surveys to customers, asking them to rate the level of effort required to schedule an appointment, communicate with staff, and get their questions answered by the chatbot. The results show a significant decrease in the level of effort required, indicating that the healthcare business has successfully reduced customer frustration.

Conclusion

By using A3 problem solving, Lean Manufacturing techniques, chatbot technology, and measuring customer experience with the Customer Effort Score (CES), the healthcare business has successfully reduced customer frustration and improved customer experience. This has resulted in increased customer satisfaction, retention, and ultimately, business success.

Hypothetical Case Study: Identifying Pain Points for a Small Restaurant Business

BACKGROUND

A small restaurant business was experiencing low customer satisfaction and decreased sales. Despite offering a wide variety of menu items and a comfortable dining environment, customers were not returning to the restaurant for future visits.

The small restaurant business has been receiving negative feedback from customers about long wait times for food and slow service. The business owner knows that addressing these frustrations is critical to retaining customers and growing the business.

Step 1: Establish the team and define the problem

The business owner forms a team consisting of the head chef, restaurant manager, and a server to address the problem. Together, they define the problem as slow service and long wait times for food.

Step 2: Describe the problem in detail

Using the 8D Tool from the Lean methodology, the team begins to describe the problem in detail. They gather data on wait times, order processing times, and customer complaints. Through their analysis, they determine that the root cause of the problem is poor communication between the kitchen and front-of-house staff.

Step 3: Containment

The team implements temporary solutions to contain the problem, such as adjusting the kitchen workflow and retraining staff on communication protocols.

Step 4: Root cause analysis

The team conducts a root cause analysis and identifies the communication breakdown between kitchen and front-of-house staff as the root cause of the problem. They implement a solution of daily meetings between the kitchen and front-of-house staff to improve communication and collaboration.

Step 5: Develop corrective actions

The team develops a corrective action plan that includes ongoing communication training for all staff and the implementation of new technology to improve communication, such as a digital order tracking system.

Step 6: Implement corrective actions

The team implements the corrective actions and monitors their effectiveness. They conduct regular check-ins with staff to ensure communication is improving and wait times are decreasing.

Step 7: Prevent recurrence

The team implements measures to prevent the problem from recurring, such as regular staff training on communication protocols and ongoing monitoring of wait times and customer feedback.

To measure the success of their efforts, the business owner implements the Net Promoter Score (NPS) survey to measure customer loyalty and satisfaction. They also track wait times and order processing times to measure efficiency improvements.

Step 8: Recognise the team

The business owner recognises the team for their hard work and dedication to improving customer satisfaction.

Conclusion

As a result of their efforts, the restaurant sees a significant increase in customer satisfaction and loyalty, leading to increased business and revenue.

Understanding the customer journey and identifying pain points is crucial for improving the overall customer experience and increasing customer satisfaction. By making changes to simplify processes and reduce pain points, the businesses improved customer satisfaction and increased sales. The case study and example provided demonstrate the importance of understanding the customer journey and identifying pain points, and the positive impact it can have on overall.

Hypothetical Case Study: Addressing Customer Frustrations for an Online Retailer

BACKGROUND:

An online retailer was experiencing high customer complaints about delivery times, which led to frustration and negative reviews. The company decided to implement strategies to address customer frustrations and turn them into delight. As a result, they decide to use Lean Manufacturing and value stream mapping to identify the root cause of the problem and make improvements to the process.

Step 1: The first step was to acknowledge the frustration. The company responded to each customer complaint with a personalised message, apologising for the delay and explaining the reasons behind it. This helped to show customers that the business was listening and taking their concerns seriously.

Step 2: The second step involved the use of Value Stream Mapping following the standard steps:

1. Define the scope: The online retailer defines the scope of the value stream map, focusing on the entire order fulfillment process, from the moment the customer places an order to the delivery of the product.
2. Map the current state: The team maps out the current state of the process, identifying all the steps, people involved, and time required to complete each step.
3. Identify wastes: The team identifies all the wastes in the current state, such as waiting times, unnecessary movements, and overproduction.

4. Map the future state: The team develops a future state map, eliminating the wastes identified in the current state and making improvements to the process.
5. Develop an action plan: The team develops an action plan to implement the changes identified in the future state map.
6. Implement changes: The team implements the changes and monitors the process to ensure that the improvements are sustained.

Step 3: To measure the impact of the changes made, the online retailer decides to use a customer satisfaction survey. They create a Customer Satisfaction Score (CSAT) survey and send it to all customers who have received a delivery after the implementation of the changes. The survey asks customers to rate their satisfaction with the delivery process on a scale of 1 to 5.

Results

After the implementation of the changes, the online retailer sees a significant improvement in their CSAT scores. The average score increases, indicating that customers are more satisfied with the delivery process. The retailer also sees a decrease in the number of customer complaints related to delivery and customer service, indicating that the improvements are having a positive impact on the overall customer experience.

Real Case Study: Tesla's Mobile Service Vans: Reducing Customer Frustration

BACKGROUND

Tesla is a company that produces electric vehicles and is known for its focus on sustainability and innovation. One of the frustrations that Tesla addressed was the inconvenience of traditional car ownership, such as having to take the car to a dealership for maintenance or repairs.

Solution

Tesla introduced mobile service vans that can come to the customer's location to perform routine maintenance and repairs. This eliminates the frustration of having to take time out of the day to bring the car to a dealership and improves the overall customer experience.

Tesla's mobile service vans are an excellent example of how the company has worked to reduce customer frustration. In the past, Tesla owners had to travel to a service centre for repairs or maintenance. With the introduction of the mobile service vans, Tesla has been able to bring the service to the customer, reducing wait times and improving the overall experience.

Tesla's mobile service vans are equipped with everything a technician would need to perform repairs or maintenance on a Tesla vehicle. The vans are equipped with diagnostic equipment, tools, and replacement parts. The technicians who operate the vans are also equipped with tablets that allow them to access customer and vehicle data, which helps to diagnose problems quickly and efficiently.

Results

As per Kyle Field in his article about Tesla's service (Field, 2019) mentions, the mobile visit "took all about 15 minutes of my time to open up the garage and chat with the tech for a few minutes. Doing the same at even the closest mechanic or dealership would take that much time just to drive there, let alone to check in and wait around for the work to be done."

Tesla used current service processes and identified areas for improvement. The company analysed the customer feedback and found opportunities to streamline the process.

Real Case Study: IKEA

Background:

IKEA is a multinational company that designs and sells ready-to-assemble furniture, kitchen appliances, and home accessories. With its focus on low prices and stylish designs, IKEA has become a popular brand worldwide. However, IKEA has also faced challenges with customer frustration, particularly with its assembly instructions and long wait times in its stores.

Solution

To address these issues, IKEA has improved operations to reduce waste, clarified team roles and used the latest technology tools to reduce customer frustration and improve the overall customer experience.

The company has adopted a similar system to the visual management from Lean philosophy, which involves sorting, standardizing, and sustaining a clean and organized space. This has helped IKEA to streamline its operations, reduce wait times in stores and improve the overall customer experience.

IKEA has encouraged staff to work together to identify and address customer frustration. These teams include representatives from customer service, product design, assembly instructions, and store operations.

From Dan's article about IKEA (Pontefract, 2016), the company instituted the "Human Resource Idea", which is described as "To give down-to-earth, straight-forward people the possibility to grow, both as individuals and in their professional roles, so that together we are strongly committed to creating a better everyday life for ourselves and our customers."

To further reduce customer frustration, IKEA has implemented several tools and technologies. These include:

- Mobile App: IKEA has developed a mobile app that allows customers to browse products, check stock availability, and even book appointments with customer service representatives. This has helped to reduce wait times in stores and improve the overall customer experience.
- Virtual Reality: IKEA has also adopted virtual reality technology to allow customers to visualize how furniture will look in their homes. This has helped to reduce customer frustration with incorrect purchases and returns.

Results

IKEA has customised many improvement methods to their specific practices and needs and has created a culture of continuous improvement that is reducing customer frustrations constantly.

By applying new technologies, IKEA was able to make it easier for customers to find what they need and reducing frustration. This resulted in improved customer satisfaction and loyalty.

Chapter Summary/Key Takeaways

- These examples demonstrate the importance of addressing customer frustrations and how to use practical steps that could apply in your company as well.
- By focusing on the customer experience and leveraging technology and innovation, these companies have created loyal customer bases and improved their profitability.
- By learning from these examples and applying similar strategies to your own businesses, you can also eliminate frustrations and improve customer satisfaction.

———————

Conclusion

———

IN CONCLUSION, WE HAVE explored the potential of frustration in the world of business and how it can be transformed into opportunities for success.

In Part I, we delved into the nature of frustration and how it can affect customer experience. We learned that frustration can be a powerful motivator for businesses to improve their products and services.

Part II focused on finding what frustrations are worth solving. It is crucial for businesses to identify the root causes of customer frustration to effectively address them. We explored the concept of frustration as an opportunity for improvement and how it can drive innovation and growth.

In Part III, we looked at how businesses can leverage technology to eliminate frustration and achieve success. From chatbots to mobile service vans, we explored emerging technologies that can help businesses streamline processes and improve customer experience. We also examined examples of frustration elimination that have proven to be successful in the business world.

Overall, this book highlights the importance of customer experience in the success of any business. By embracing frustration as an opportunity for growth, businesses can improve their products and services, increase customer satisfaction, and drive innovation. Through the application of lean manufacturing principles, problem-solving strategies, and the implementation of emerging technologies, businesses can transform frustration into delight and achieve success in today's competitive market.

It is my hope that this book has provided you with valuable insights and tools to help you achieve your business and personal goals. Here I encourage you start implementing some of these techniques in your own operations. If you have any further questions or would like to learn more about how these techniques can be applied to your business, please do not hesitate to contact me. Thank you for reading.

References

CAPITAL, F. (FIFOCAPITAL.co.nz). Richard Branson: making the World better. Retrieved from https://fifocapital.co.nz/richard-branson-making-world-better/

Cornfield, G. (2021, May). Designing Customer Journeys for the Post-Pandemic World. Retrieved from https://hbr.org/2021/05/designing-customer-journeys-for-the-post-pandemic-world

Dorsey, M., Segall, D., & Temkin, B. (n.d.). ROI of Customer Experience, 2020. Qualtrics XM Institute.

Estrada, E. J. (2023). Sorry About the Wait - A lean guide to reducing wait times and improve customer experience.

Field, K. (2019). Clean Technica. Retrieved from cleantechnica.com: https://cleantechnica.com/2019/08/17/the-future-of-teslas-mobile-service-fleet/

Pontefract, D. (2016). How IKEA Delights Its Customers. Retrieved from www.forbes.com: https://www.forbes.com/sites/danpontefract/2016/06/08/how-ikea-delights-its-customers/?sh=1e29fc7d3ca4

Press, O. U. (2021). Oxford University Press. Retrieved from In Oxford Learner's Dictionaries: https://www.oxfordlearnersdictionaries.com/

Sinek, S. (n.d.). Find Your Why. In S. Sinek, Find Your Why.

Smith, M. (n.d.). 107 Customer Service Statistics and Facts You Shouldn't Ignore. Retrieved from https://www.helpscout.com/75-customer-service-facts-quotes-statistics

Acknowledgments

WRITING A BOOK IS A challenging effort, and this project would not have been possible without the support and assistance of many people. I would like to express my sincere gratitude to the following people:

First and foremost, a heartfelt thank you to all my family for their genuine support throughout this project. Their patience, encouragement, and understanding were invaluable in making this book a reality.

I would like to express my sincere gratitude to Rocio Ampie for creating such a beautiful cover for my book. Your creativity and attention to detail have made this book stand out and I am truly grateful for your hard work and dedication

I would also like to thank my colleagues and mentors along the years, who provided me guidance and expertise throughout my professional development to be able to write this book. Their insights and perspectives were instrumental in shaping the content of this book.

Special thanks to the editors and publishing team who worked tirelessly to bring this book to fruition. Their professionalism and attention to detail ensured that the final product was of the highest quality.

Finally, I would like to express gratitude to the readers of this book, to you who have taken the time to engage with these ideas and concepts presented here. It is your curiosity and dedication that inspires me to continue exploring the world of Lean Manufacturing and business process improvement.

Thank you all for your contributions and support. This book would not have been possible without your help.

Don't miss out!

Visit the website below and you can sign up to receive emails whenever Eduardo J. Estrada publishes a new book. There's no charge and no obligation.

https://books2read.com/r/B-A-HFWX-MJVHC

Connecting independent readers to independent writers.

Also by Eduardo J. Estrada

The F... Word Advantage
Sorry About the Wait

About the Author

Eduardo J. Estrada is an experienced Industrial Engineer with a professional background in Sustainability, Quality and Lean management. With over 15 years of experience, the author has worked extensively in the manufacturing industry, identifying, and implementing process improvements to enhance efficiency and reduce waste.

The author has been recognized for his contributions to sustainability and operations excellence, having been instrumental in winning awards for the companies where he has worked. Currently residing in Australia with his family, the author enjoys spending his free time travelling, cycling, reading, and working on improving business processes.

With a passion for continuous improvement and a deep understanding of Lean Manufacturing tools, the author brings a wealth of knowledge and expertise to this book. Through his work, the author aims to help organizations reduce wait times and queues, improve customer experience, and drive business success.

If you want to learn more about these topics or would like to start a conversation, you can reach out at: theleanmate@outlook.com

Ingram Content Group UK Ltd.
Milton Keynes UK
UKHW020930260423
420810UK00016B/664

9 798215 100622